How Small Is Small?
Comparing Body Parts

Vic Parker

LIBRARY

Chicago, Illinois

www.heinemannraintree.com
Visit our website to find out more information about Heinemann-Raintree books.

To order:
☎ Phone 888-454-2279
💻 Visit www.heinemannraintree.com to browse our catalog and order online.

Edited by Nancy Dickmann, Rebecca Rissman, and Sian Smith
Designed by Victoria Allen
Picture research by Hannah Taylor
Original illustrations © Capstone Global Library 2011
Original illustrations by Victoria Allen
Production by Victoria Fitzgerald
Originated by Dot Gradations Ltd
Printed and bound in China by South China Printing Company Ltd

14 13 12 11 10
10 9 8 7 6 5 4 3 2 1

Library of Congress Cataloging-in-Publication Data
Parker, Victoria.
    How small is small?:comparing body parts / Vic Parker.
        p. cm.—(Measuring and comparing)
    Includes bibliographical references and index.
    ISBN 978-1-4329-3960-1 (hc)—ISBN 978-1-4329-3968-7 (pb) 1. Body size—Juvenile literature. 2. Weights and measures.—Juvenile literature. I. Title.
    QM27.P267 2011
    591.4′1—dc22   2010000938

Acknowledgments
The author and publisher are grateful to the following for permission to reproduce copyright material: Alamy Images pp. 7 (© John Bower London), 24 (© Radius Images); © Capstone Publishers pp. 5, 8, 9, 12, 26, 27 (Karon Dubke); istockphoto pp. 18, 14 (© Heather Down), 20 (© Ron Chapple Stock), 22 (© Helmar Niemeijer); Photolibrary pp. 6, 10 (Kevin Dodge); shutterstock pp. 4 (© clickit), 11 (© ZouZou), 16 (© Racheal Grazias).

Photographs used to create silhouettes: shutterstock, child (© Slobodan Zivkovic), man (© Augusto Cabral), baby (© Toshik), leg (© Robert Adrian Hillman), hand (© Michael D. Brown), foot (© andrisr).

Cover photograph of a boy holding his fingers up to indicate a short distance reproduced with permission of Corbis (Simon Jarratt).

Every effort has been made to contact copyright holders of material reproduced in this book. Any omissions will be rectified in subsequent printings if notice is given to the publisher.

Contents

Words appearing in the text in bold, **like this**, are explained in the glossary.

What Is Small?

When we talk about something being small, we mean that it is small compared to something else. For example, a baby elephant is small compared to its mother.

A baby elephant is shorter and narrower than its mother.

It is not always easy to figure out which thing is the smallest. To decide if one thing is smaller than another, we often have to look at more than one measurement.

Is the apple or the flower smaller? The apple is shorter, but the flower is narrower.

Height, Length, and Width

When we measure an object, we can look at its **height**, **length**, or **width**. The height of something is how tall it is. An object can be tall or short.

Some basketball players are taller than others.

height

The length of something is how long it is. An object can be long or short. The width of something is how far it is from side to side. An object can be wide or narrow.

A car is much wider than a bicycle.

width

length

Measuring Size

We measure something's **length**, **height**, and **width** to find out how small it is. We measure big sizes in feet (ft.) and smaller sizes in inches (in.).

We can use rulers to measure small objects like these toy animals.

You can use different tools to measure length, height, and width. You can use a ruler, tape measure, or measuring stick.

A tape measure can measure longer things than a ruler can.

The Human Body

The human body is made up of many parts. Some parts are smaller than others. A hand is smaller than an arm. A finger is smaller than a foot. Even parts inside you can be big or small.

Our body parts are different shapes and sizes.

A person's body changes size during his or her lifetime. Body parts grow as a person changes from a baby to an adult. Some body parts, such as hair and fingernails, never stop growing!

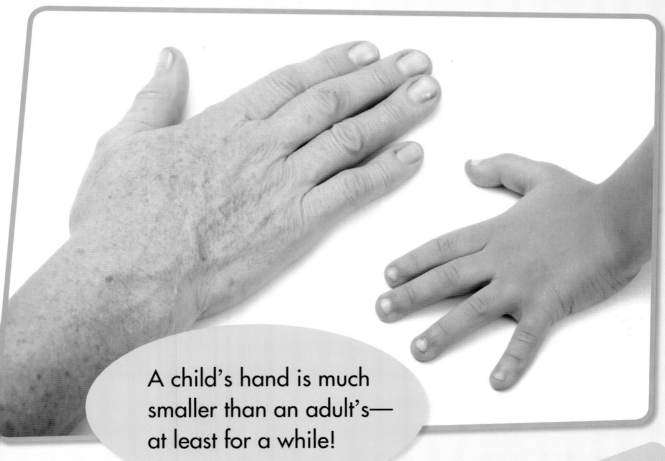

A child's hand is much smaller than an adult's— at least for a while!

How Tall Are You?

Have you ever measured how tall you are? Compared to a younger brother or sister, you might be tall. But compared to most adults, you might be short.

You can measure your **height** on a wall chart.

A fully grown man might be about 5 feet, 10 inches (or 70 total inches) tall, but a child is shorter. An eight-year-old child might only be about 4 feet, 2 inches (or 50 total inches) tall.

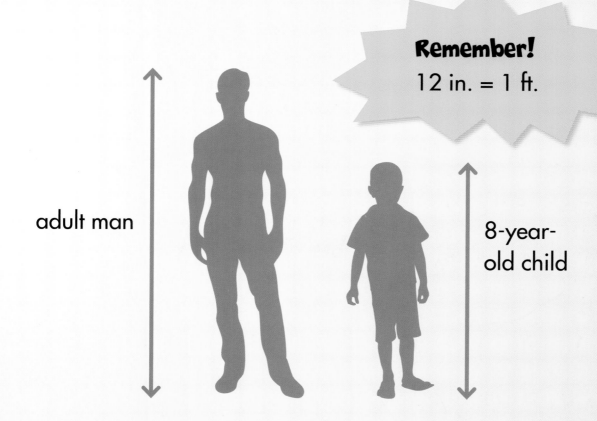

Remember!
12 in. = 1 ft.

adult man

8-year-old child

What is shorter than a child? ➡

A Baby

A baby is much shorter than a child. Babies are very small when they are developing inside their mothers. Once they are born, they grow quickly.

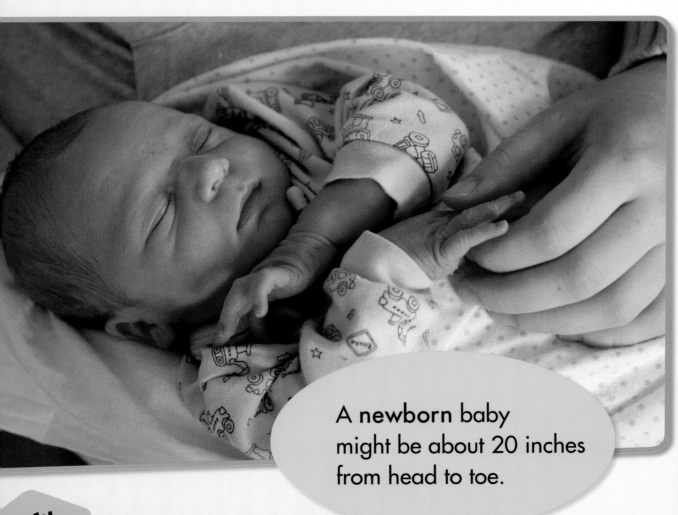

A **newborn** baby might be about 20 inches from head to toe.

By the time a baby is one year old, he or she might be around 2 feet, 6 inches (or 30 total inches) tall. A one-year-old is a little more than half as tall as an eight-year-old child.

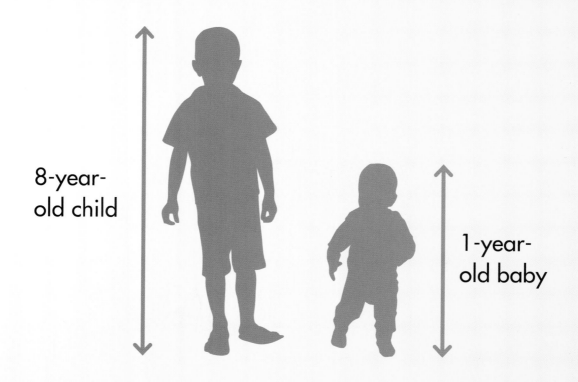

8-year-old child

1-year-old baby

A baby is short and small. What else is small? ➡

How Long Is Your Leg?

Some body parts are long. Have you ever measured your leg? Compared to your whole body, your leg is short. But your foot is even shorter.

Legs help us walk and run.

Your leg might be 28 inches long. Your foot could be about 8 inches long. It would take three and a half of your feet to be as long as your leg.

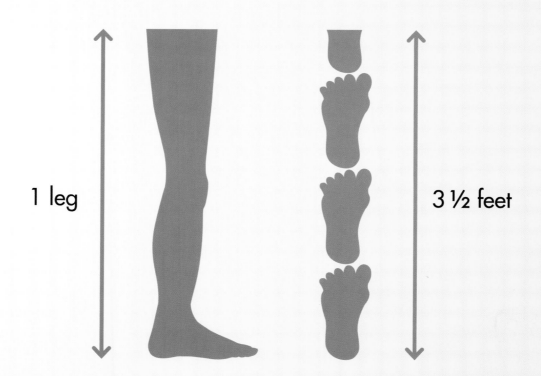

1 leg

3 ½ feet

What is shorter than your foot? ➡

Your Toes

Your toes are shorter than your foot. Toes are important for helping you **balance**. They also help you push off from the ground when you walk.

Toes are different sizes. For many people, their big toe is the longest.

Your big toe might be about 1½ inches long.
It would take more than five big toes to be as
long as your foot.

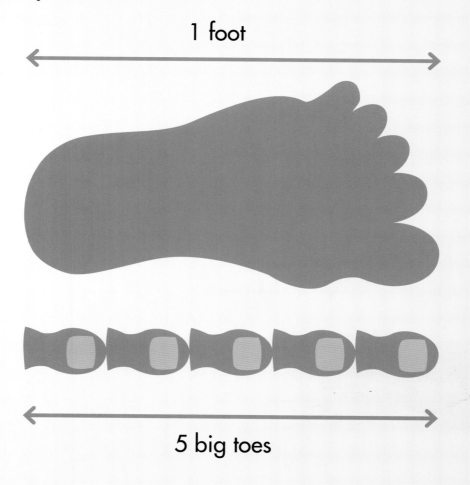

1 foot

5 big toes

**A big toe is short and small.
What else is small?** →

How Wide Are Your Shoulders?

Some body parts are wide. Have you ever measured the **width** of your shoulders? For many people they are the widest part of the body. Your hand is much narrower.

You use your shoulders in activities such as throwing.

Your shoulders might be about 13 inches wide. When you spread out your fingers, your hand might be about 6 inches wide. It would take more than two hands to be as wide as your shoulders.

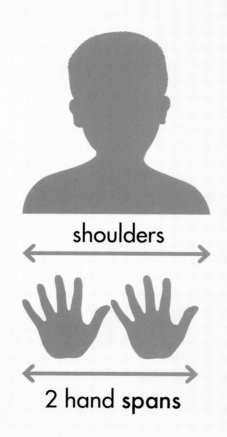

shoulders

2 hand spans

What is narrower than your hand?

Your Thumbnail

Fingernails are narrower than your hand.
Fingernails are hard to **protect** our fingers.
They also help us to pick things up.

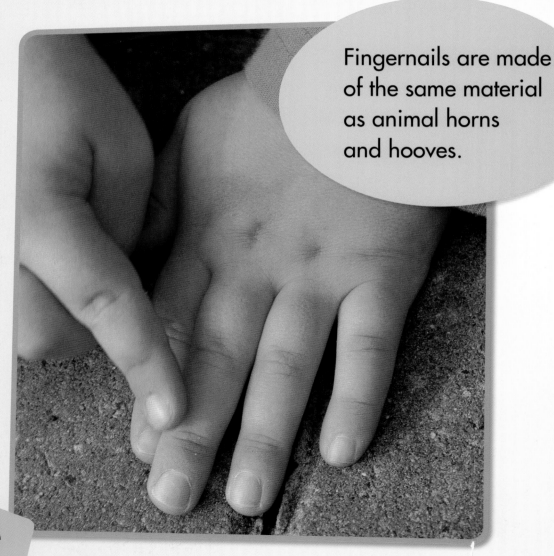

Fingernails are made of the same material as animal horns and hooves.

Your thumbnail is the widest of your fingernails. Even so, it is probably only about half an inch wide. It would take just over 12 thumbnails to be as wide as your hand.

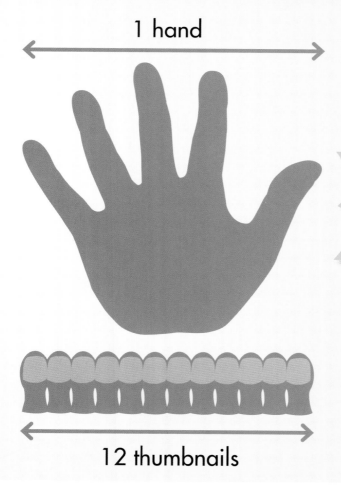

1 hand

12 thumbnails

Remember this to help with the quiz on p28.

What is narrower than your thumbnail? ➡️

A Freckle

A freckle is narrower than your thumbnail.
Freckles are small, dark spots that some people
have on their bodies. Freckles can get darker
if you spend time in the sun.

If your parents have
freckles, you are likely
to have freckles, too.

Freckles are tiny—only about ¹⁄₂₅ of an inch wide. It may take 13 freckles, laid side to side, to be as wide as your thumbnail.

1 thumbnail

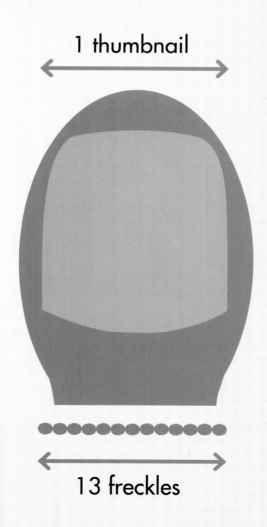

13 freckles

Measuring Activity

Things you will need: an old sheet, a marker, a tray of paint, a floor it is safe to use paint on, a helper, and old towels and water for cleaning.

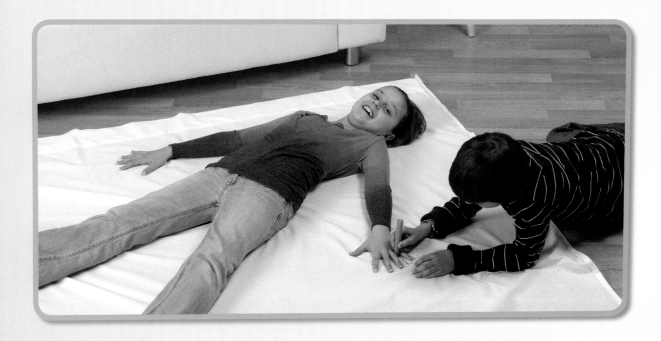

① Spread out the sheet so it is flat and unwrinkled on the floor. Lie down on it with your legs apart and your arms away from your sides. Ask your helper to draw around your body with the marker. When you stand up, you should have an outline of your body on the sheet.

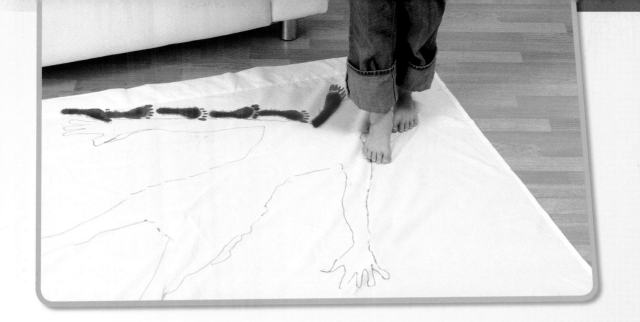

(2) Put your tray of paint close to the outline of your arm and step into the tray with bare feet. Make sure that the bottoms of your feet are covered with paint. Carefully put one foot onto the outline of your arm, so your heel lines up with the start of your wrist. Walk heel-to-toe up your arm, then step off onto an old towel.

(3) Do the same with other body parts, such as your leg, your back, and your whole body **length**.

Find out: How many lengths of your foot does it take to make up your other body parts?

Size Quiz and Facts

Units for measuring height, length, and width

Small sizes are measured in inches (in.).
Big sizes are measured in feet (ft.).

Quiz

1. What unit would you use to measure the **width** of a thumbnail?
   a) inches   b) feet

2. What unit would you use to measure the **height** of a real giraffe?
   a) inches   b) feet

3. What unit would you use to measure the **length** of a cat?
   a) inches b) feet

Answers: 1 = a   2 = b   3 = a

28

> **Remember**
>
> 12 inches (in.) = 1 foot (ft.)

Small Facts

- The colored part of your eye (the **iris**), including the black part (the **pupil**), is about half an inch wide. But the pupil can become bigger or smaller, depending on how much light there is to see by.

- The smallest **bone** in the human body is inside the ear. It is called the **stapes** (or stirrup) and it is just $1/10$ of an inch long.

- An eight-year-old's tongue measures around 4 inches long.

- The width of a hair on a human's head is tiny. It would take about 10 human head hairs to make up the width of one freckle.

Glossary

balance being able to stand up without falling over

bone body part that is stiff and strong. Bones are inside your body. They hold your body up and give it shape.

height how tall or high something is

iris colored part of your eye

length how long something is

newborn baby that is just a day or a few days old

protect keep safe

pupil round, black opening in the middle of your eye. Light comes into your eye through the pupil.

span how far something is from one end to another. Your hand span is the measurement of how far it is from the tip of your thumb to the tip of your little finger on your stretched-out hand.

stapes bone inside your ear. The stapes is the smallest bone in the human body.

width how wide something is or how much it measures from side to side

Find Out More

Books

Hewitt, Sally. *How Big Is It? (Measuring series)* North Mankato, MN: Stargazer, 2008.

Royston, Angela. *Human Growth. (My World of Science series)* Chicago: Heinemann Library, 2009.

Taylor, Barbara. *My Best Book of the Human Body.* New York: Kingfisher, 2008.

Web Sites

www.kidshealth.org/kid/htbw
Find out all about fingernails and other small body parts on this website.

www.funbrain.com/measure/
Try this simple quiz, which asks you to identify the correct measurements in inches.

Index